WHAT IS MY BATHROOM MADE OF?

Written by ALEX HALL

MATERIALS AT HOME

maple bay

Library of Congress Control Number:
The Library of Congress Control Number is available on the Library of Congress website.

ISBN
979-8-89359-428-7 (library bound)
979-8-89359-448-5 (paperback)
979-8-89359-486-7 (epub)
979-8-89359-468-3 (hosted ebook)

Printed in the United States of America
Mankato, MN
012026

sales@northstareditions.com
888-417-0195

Written by:
Alex Hall

Edited by:
Noah Leatherland

Designed by:
Amy Li

PHOTO CREDITS

ALL IMAGES ARE COURTESY OF SHUTTERSTOCK.COM, UNLESS OTHERWISE STATED.
Recurring – fire_fly, xnova. Cover – Alhovik, JOJOSTUDIO, mStudioVector, picoStudio, The Studio, Inside Creative House, Jamroen_Photo Background, New Africa, Anton Starikov. 2–3 – Ground Picture. 4–5 – PeopleImages.com - Yuri A, Phawat. 6–7 – AYDO8, New Africa, Tanya Sid. 8–9 – donatas1205, LIGHTITUP, patpitchaya. 10–11 – Pixel-Shot, xpixel, Josh brown photography. 12–13 – Pixel-Shot, almo Creative, New Africa. 14–15 – Regreto, PeopleImages.com - Yuri A, New Africa. 16–17 – RHJPhtotos, Toyakisphoto, Suzanne Tucker. 18–19 – K'Nub, Melnikov Dmitriy, gresei. 20–21 – Businesspictures, s-ts, TORSupachai, nuruddean, New Africa. 22–23 – Procreators, Sklo Studio.

CONTENTS

Words that look like this can be found in the glossary on page 24.

WHAT ARE MATERIALS?

The things that you can see and touch are called objects. There are many objects in your bathroom. Objects are made of materials. Materials can be natural or human-made.

Metals are a natural material. Most are found in the ground.

All materials have properties. Properties are ways of describing what something is like. Materials can be soft, hard, sturdy, or bendy. There are many different properties that materials can have.

MY TOILET AND MY BATHTUB

My toilet is made of porcelain. Porcelain is a type of ceramic. It is a durable, human-made material. It is strong enough to hold a person's weight without breaking.

PORCELAIN

My bathtub is also made of porcelain. Porcelain is water resistant. Water can't easily pass through or damage it. Porcelain stops your bathwater from leaking everywhere.

FACT:
Porcelain is smooth, which makes it easy to clean.

MY FAUCETS

My faucets are made of brass. Brass is made from natural metals. It's made by mixing other metals together. Brass is durable. It can handle powerful jets of water.

Water and air weaken most metals over time. Brass weakens slower than other metals. So, brass can stay safe to carry water for a long time.

MY WINDOW

GLASS

My bathroom window is made of glass. Glass is human-made from natural materials. It is transparent. Light can travel through it. This is why you can see through most windows.

My other bathroom window is made of obscure glass. Obscure glass still lets in light, but you can't see through it. This keeps the bathroom **private**.

Does your bathroom have obscure glass windows?

MY TOILET PAPER

My toilet paper is made of soft, thin paper. Paper comes from wood. Wood is a natural material. The wood is turned into a gooey pulp. Then the pulp is dried to make paper.

PAPER

Toilet paper is weak and can be ripped into small pieces. It is also easy to break down. These properties are why you can flush toilet paper to get rid of it.

MY TOWEL

COTTON

My towel is made of cotton. Cotton is a natural material. Cotton is soft and gentle on your skin.

Cotton towels are absorbent. They can soak up water. This is why we use cotton towels to dry our hands and bodies after washing.

MY MIRROR

My mirror is made of glass. You can't see through a mirror. Mirrors have a shiny metal under the glass, such as silver or aluminum.

FACT:
The glass in a mirror is thin and can break easily.

Light can pass through the glass, but it can't pass through the metal. The metal reflects the light. This lets you see yourself in the mirror. This is called your reflection.

MY TOOTHBRUSH

My toothbrush is made of plastic. Plastic is a human-made material. The bristles on a toothbrush are made from a plastic called nylon. Nylon bristles are thin and bendy to help clean between your teeth.

BRISTLES

PLASTIC

Some people use electric toothbrushes. Electric toothbrushes have a motor inside. The motor spins the bristles. This helps clean your teeth.

SPOT THE MATERIALS

Which of these objects is made of plastic?

SHOWERHEAD

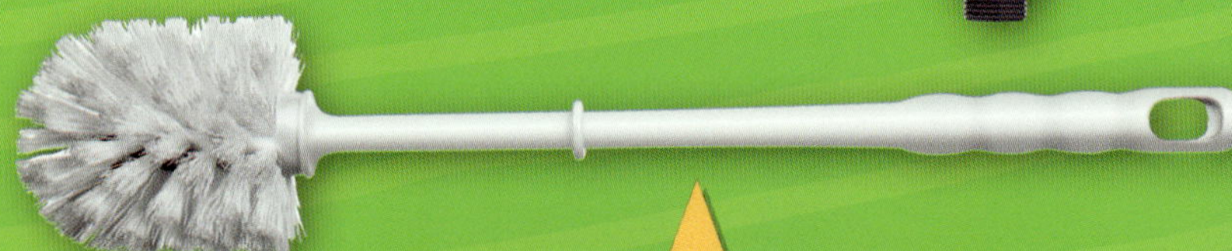

TOILET BRUSH

SINK BASIN

Only the toilet brush is made of plastic. The shower head is made of metal, and the sink is made of porcelain.

Which of these objects is made of cotton?

BATHROOM TILES

SHAMPOO BOTTLE

BATH MAT

Only the bath mat is made of cotton. The bathroom tiles are made of porcelain, and the shampoo bottle is made of plastic.

WHAT IS IN YOUR BATHROOM?

There are many different materials in our bathrooms. They were chosen because of their useful properties. Without these properties, the materials would not be able to do their jobs.

The objects in your bathroom might be made of different materials than mine. Look at something in your bathroom. Do you know what it is made of? Why do you think that material was used?

GLOSSARY

DESCRIBING	saying what something is like
DURABLE	not easily broken or worn out
ELECTRIC	able to work by using energy
NATURAL	found in nature and not made by people
PRIVATE	hidden from others and kept to oneself
REFLECTS	bounces back light, heat, or sound

INDEX